When Will the Sun Go Out?

and other strange solar system science

By Isabel Thomas

Contents

The solar system

What is it?

Everything that **orbits** the Sun is part of our solar system. It's a very strange place where nothing is what it seems. Earth may look enormous from where you're standing, but on a solar system scale it's just a tiny ball of rock zooming around the Sun.

Our solar system is made up of eight planets, five dwarf planets, dozens of moons and hundreds of thousands of smaller chunks of rock, metal and ice.

How did it all start?

Our solar system is very old. It's older than your teacher! It's even older than your great-great-great grandparents. Think 4,567,000,000 birthday candles! A few billion years ago, the solar system was full of objects smashing, crashing and breaking chunks off each other.*

*Rocket to page 14 to discover how a massive crash formed the Moon!

Name: **Galileo Galilei**

Dates: 1564–1642

Job: **Space scientist**

What would happen if you made an amazing scientific discovery? Would you get top marks from your teacher? Probably, but not if you were Italian **astronomer** Galileo in the 1600s. His discoveries got him arrested and locked up because people didn't believe in them!

Galileo loved doing experiments to find out how the world worked. When he heard about a new invention called a telescope, he built his own. While other people were busy spying on their neighbours, Galileo pointed his telescope at planets in the night sky. He found proof that the planets orbit the Sun. At that time, most people believed that everything in space travelled around Earth. Galileo's ideas got him into big trouble, but many of his ideas turned out to be right!

Galileo was put on trial and kept under house arrest for the rest of his life.

Starring ... the Sun

How many suns can you see in the sky?

It depends if you look during the day or night. The Sun is a star, just like the thousands of other stars that you can see at night. The Sun is much, much closer to us than these other stars, so it looks much, much bigger. It lies at the centre of our solar system.

The star of our solar system

Like all stars, the Sun releases huge amounts of energy into space. This energy zooms out across the solar system, bringing heat and light to Earth. The Sun is 150,000,000 kilometres away. Light travels so fast that the rays of sunlight hitting you now only left the Sun's surface eight minutes ago!

When will the Sun go out?

Stars don't burn forever. Eventually they run out of fuel and swell up. Small, boring stars cool down and shrink, but the biggest stars explode! Our Sun has five billion years left – more than enough time to get your homework done!

Never look at the Sun directly, or through any kind of binoculars or telescope. You could damage your eyes forever, and even go blind.

4

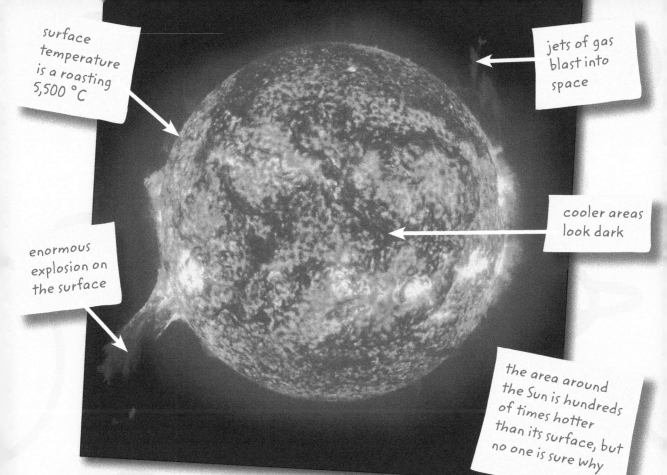

surface temperature is a roasting 5,500 °C

jets of gas blast into space

cooler areas look dark

enormous explosion on the surface

the area around the Sun is hundreds of times hotter than its surface, but no one is sure why

Top 5: ways Earth needs the Sun

1 It lights and heats our planet.

2 It allows plants to grow, giving us food and the oxygen we breathe.

3 It causes weather, keeping warm and cool air moving around the planet.

4 It powers the water cycle, supplying us with fresh water.

5 It is the original source of most of our power, from fossil fuels to wind and wave power.

Great balls of rock!

The Sun is pointless!

The strange thing about stars is that they're not star-shaped. The Sun is actually a sphere, which means that it has no edges or points at all. In fact, it's shaped more like a massive tennis ball (without the fuzz).

Ant's eye view

Earth and the other planets in our solar system are spherical too. It doesn't feel like we're walking around on a ball, because the Earth is so big we can't see the ground curving.

In the wrong

People once thought that Earth was as flat as a pancake! They began to realise the strange truth when they noticed that the bottom of ships disappeared first as they sailed away. This could only happen if the Earth's surface was curved.

When humans invented spaceships to zoom high above Earth's surface, they saw the ball-shaped Earth for themselves.

Try this

Can you work out how big the planets are compared to each other?

What you need:

- some ball-shaped objects
- a ruler
- a pencil and some paper

What to do:

1 Find ball-shaped objects with the diameters shown in the chart below. Try looking in the kitchen, garden, an arts and crafts cupboard, and toy box. Carry your ruler with you.

2 Label each object with the name of the solar system object it represents. Line all the objects up in order (see the table below) and compare their sizes.

3 At this scale, the Sun would be one metre wide! Can you find a ball-shaped object to represent the Sun?

Object	Scaled-down diameter
Mercury	3 mm
Venus	9 mm
Earth	9 mm
Moon	2 mm
Mars	5 mm
Jupiter	10.2 cm
Saturn	8.5 cm
Uranus	3.4 cm
Neptune	3.3 cm

Hint: don't forget, the real objects are 1.4 billion times bigger than your models!

Day and night

Who turned out the light?

As you get used to the idea of balancing on a gigantic ball, let's add some even stranger solar system science to the mix. Objects leave shadows when it is sunny because they block the sunlight and stop it hitting the ground. At night, no sunlight hits the ground at all. Everything is in shadow, and the object blocking the light is Earth itself!

Give the Sun a high-five!

Pick a sunny day, stand facing the Sun, and hold up your hand so sunlight strikes your palm. The back of your hand is in shadow. This is because it's pointing away from the Sun. You can light up different parts of your hand by turning it.

Remember not to look at the Sun directly!

In a spin

Our planet also turns in space, so that sunlight hits different parts of it at different times. Every 24 hours, Earth spins once on its **axis**. This spinning causes day and night.

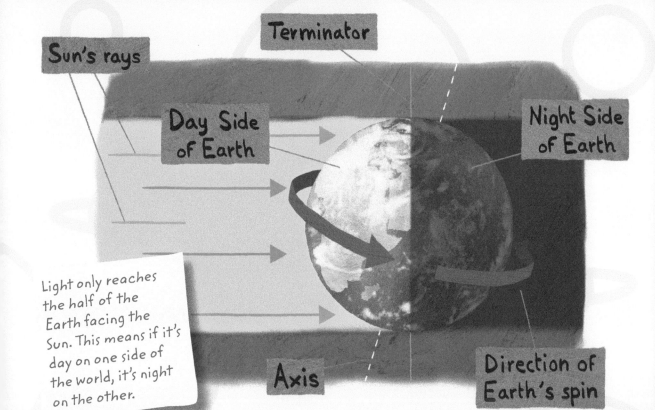

Sun's rays

Terminator

Day Side of Earth

Night Side of Earth

Light only reaches the half of the Earth facing the Sun. This means if it's day on one side of the world, it's night on the other.

Axis

Direction of Earth's spin

In the wrong

During the day, the Sun seems to move across the sky. Many ancient folk thought that the Sun was moving around the Earth but it's actually Earth that's moving! As Earth spins, the Sun appears to rise in the east and set in the west.

terminator

The line between day and night is called the terminator! As Earth spins, the terminator moves across the planet. Everyone living just to the left of this line is about to experience dawn.

Years and seasons

Stop the planet – I want to get off!

As well as turning on its axis, Earth is also orbiting the Sun at 108,000 kilometres per hour (67,000 mph). That's 1,000 times faster than a family car travels on the motorway!

How many days in a year... really?

The time a planet takes to make one journey around the Sun is called a year. Each of your birthdays is really a celebration that you've survived another journey around the solar system! Earth is pretty fast – it takes 365 (and a bit) days to orbit the Sun once*. Every four years, all the extra 'bits' are added up to make an extra day on 29th February.

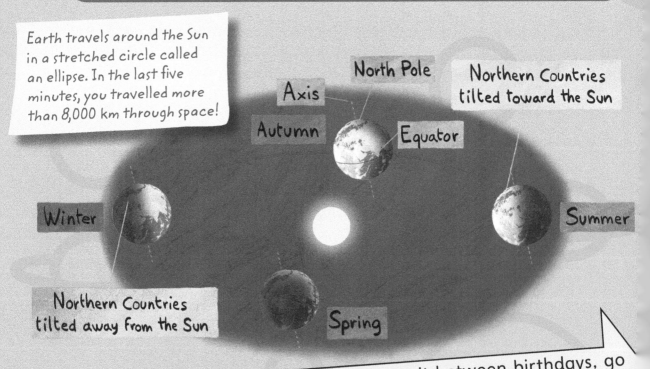

Earth travels around the Sun in a stretched circle called an ellipse. In the last five minutes, you travelled more than 8,000 km through space!

North Pole

Axis

Northern Countries tilted toward the Sun

Autumn

Equator

Winter

Summer

Northern Countries tilted away from the Sun

Spring

*If you think 365 days is a long time to wait between birthdays, go to page 24 to find out where years are 204,400 Earth days long!

Why isn't the Sun as hot in winter?

The seasons make it more fun to live on Earth: crunchy autumn leaves, winter snowball fights, baby animals in spring and hot summer days. The seasons happen because our planet is a bit wonky!

Earth is tilted on its axis. As it travels around the Sun, the area we live in tilts away from the Sun during the winter months, and towards the Sun during the summer months. This causes shorter, colder days in winter and longer, hotter days in summer.

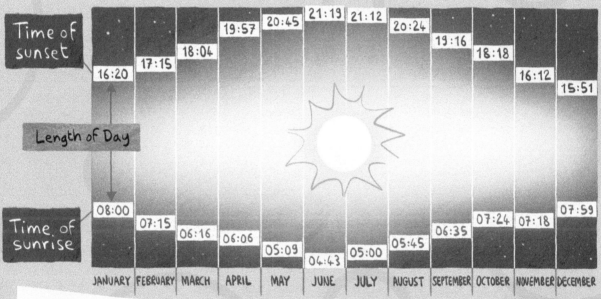

Time of sunset

19:57 | 20:45 | 21:19 | 21:12 | 20:24 | 19:16 | 18:18 | 16:12 | 15:51

18:04 | 17:15 | 16:20

Length of Day

Time of sunrise

08:00 | 07:15 | 06:16 | 06:06 | 05:09 | 04:43 | 05:00 | 05:45 | 06:35 | 07:24 | 07:18 | 07:59

JANUARY | FEBRUARY | MARCH | APRIL | MAY | JUNE | JULY | AUGUST | SEPTEMBER | OCTOBER | NOVEMBER | DECEMBER

This graph shows the time of sunrise and sunset in London on the 15th day of each month. The gap between the sunrise line and the sunset line shows the length of the day at that time of year.

When do the days start to get longer? And when do days start to get shorter?

The mysterious Moon

Nice but dim

The Moon orbits Earth, and is our nearest neighbour in space. Although it is much closer to us than the Sun, the Moon is not as bright in the sky. It doesn't make its own light like a star. Instead, the Moon reflects the light from the Sun.

Shape-shifting

As neighbours go, the Moon is very strange. Every night it seems to change shape and sometimes it disappears altogether! These different shapes are called the **phases** of the Moon. People were really confused before scientists discovered what was going on.

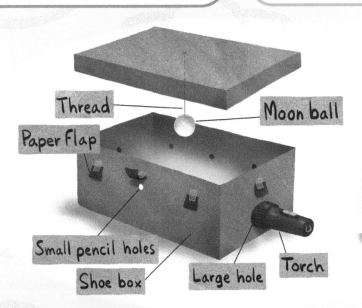

Thread

Moon ball

Paper Flap

Small pencil holes

Shoe box

Large hole

Torch

Follow the instructions in the 'Try this!' box on page 13 to make this model which shows the phases of the Moon.

Full moon or banana?

Of course, the Moon doesn't really change shape – it's a solid sphere of rock. Like Earth, only one side of the Moon is lit up by the Sun at any time. As the Moon orbits Earth, we see different parts of that sunlit side.

Try this!

Can you make a model that shows all the phases of the Moon?

What you need:

- an empty shoebox
- some black paint
- a pencil and scissors
- a large piece of black paper
- some cotton thread
- some sticky tape
- a polystyrene or foam ball
- a small torch

What to do:

1 Paint the shoebox black inside (including the lid) and let it dry.

2 Use a pencil to poke eight holes in the box, in the places shown in the picture on page 12. Stick a small flap of black paper over each hole.

3 Cut a larger hole at one end of the box, to fit the end of the torch through.

4 Cut a piece of thread just over half the height of the shoebox. Stick one end of the thread to the ball and one to the centre of the lid.

5 Put the lid on the shoebox so the ball hangs in the centre of the box. Shine a torch through the large hole, lighting up one side of your Moon like the Sun does.

6 Lift each flap one at a time and peek through the holes to view the Moon from different positions.

Visiting the Moon

Walking on the Moon

The Moon is the only other solar system object that humans have visited. In the 1960s and 1970s, 12 astronauts walked on the surface and had lots of fun hopping, kicking rocks and even hitting golf balls, just to see what happened!

A bumpy start

Scientists think that the Moon was formed when a giant **asteroid** the size of Mars smashed into Earth!* Massive amounts of dust and rubble were thrown into space and trapped in orbit around Earth. The lumps began to collide, slowly gathering into a ball that became the Moon.

Asteroid

Earth

*Go to page 26 to find out more about destructive asteroids.

A real pounding!

After it was formed, the Moon was pounded by flying space rocks, cracking the crust and cratering the surface. Today the Moon is covered in a thick layer of dust and rubble.

In the wrong

Some ancient astronomers thought the dark areas on the Moon were water. These 'seas and oceans' were given watery names like 'The Marsh of Decay' and 'The Lake of Death'. They are actually huge areas of solid lava, from ancient volcanoes.

There is no wind on the Moon, so it will take a million years or more for footprints and buggy tracks to disappear from its dusty surface.

Strange...

As the Moon orbits Earth, it also spins on its own axis. This keeps the same side of the Moon facing Earth all the time. Spacecraft have flown around the Moon, revealing that the far side is ... pretty similar to the one we can see. Oh well!

... but true

Nasty neighbours

What else is out there?

Bored with the Moon's shape-shifting? Earth has some even more interesting neighbours in space – the seven other planets of our solar system. Some are a lot bigger than Earth, but they are all tiny compared to the Sun.

Where can I see them?

The other planets all orbit the Sun at different distances. Five of them, Mercury, Venus, Mars, Jupiter and Saturn, can be spotted from Earth without a telescope.*

Jupiter

Saturn

Mars

Venus

Mercury

The planets look like stars in the night sky. Venus is the brightest, and the easiest to spot. Look for it in the early morning and early evening.

*Blast to page 18 and 20 to find out about these deadly planets.

Try this!

Can you make a model of the solar system?

What you need:

- some modelling clay
- nine lolly sticks
- some coloured paper and pens
- a large outside area
- a trundle wheel or metre stick

What to do:

1 Make nine small balls of clay to represent the Sun and each planet. Use the lolly sticks and coloured paper to make a name flag to stick in the top of each one. This will help you to see them from a distance.

2 In a large outdoor area, place the Sun on the ground. Use the chart to measure the scaled-down distance to Mercury, and put your model of Mercury on the ground.

3 Carry on placing planets until you run out of space. You can double back on yourself to fit in all the planets.

Solar system object	Real distance from Sun (km)	Scaled-down distance from Sun (metres)
Sun	0	0
Mercury	58 million	2.1
Venus	108 million	3.9
Earth	150 million	5.5
Mars	228 million	8.3
Jupiter	778 million	28.4
Saturn	1,430 million	52
Uranus	2,870 million	104.8
Neptune	4,500 million	164.2

The rocky planets

Heavy metal

The rocky planets (Mercury, Venus, Earth and Mars) are the closest planets to the Sun. They are pretty speedy for lumps of rock and metal. The closer they are to the Sun, the faster they move around it.

Happy New Year ... again!

Mercury, Venus and Mars have days and years, but they are very different from those on Earth. Mercury zips around the Sun in just 88 Earth days, but spins on its axis very, very slowly. This gives Mercury a strange calendar, with 1.5 Mercury days in one Mercury year!

Planet spotting

The rocky planets were first spotted thousands of years ago. Try looking out for them yourself (if you can't spot Earth, it might be time for an eye test!). Venus is the brightest – not because it's closest to Earth, but because its thick clouds reflect lots of the Sun's light.

Mars has two moons called Phobos and Deimos, meaning 'fear' and 'terror'!

A closer look

Around 50 years ago, humans started sending robot **space probes** to get a closer look at the rocky planets. Mars is the top destination because its volcanoes and signs of water mean there might be some kind of alien life on the planet (think tiny microbes, rather than little green men).

Several **rovers** have driven around the surface of Mars, collecting information to beam back to Earth.

Mercury is the solar system's punch bag. It is covered by craters caused by pieces of space rock crashing into it.

Strange...

Mercury is a silent planet. It does not have a proper **atmosphere** for sound to travel through.

... but true

The gas giants

Taking it slowly

Compared to the rocky planets, Jupiter, Saturn, Uranus and Neptune are slow-moving monsters. Neptune takes 165 Earth years to orbit the Sun. Only one Neptune year has passed since the planet was discovered in 1846.

That sinking feeling

These huge planets are made mostly of gas, so they don't have solid surfaces. They are also much colder than the rocky planets, because they are further from the Sun's warmth.

Are we nearly there yet?

So many moons surround each gas giant, it's hard to keep count. Jupiter has at least 63! Space probes have been sent to poke around all the gas giants and their moons. Some of the things they have discovered have knocked the socks off space scientists!

Great Red Spot

Jupiter's Great Red Spot is a huge hurricane bigger than our planet! Humans first spotted it more than 300 years ago.

The gas giants all have rings. If you zoomed in on Saturn's rings, you'd see zillions of chunks of ice, sparkling in the Sun's light.

Top 5: strange moons

1 Ganymede is the largest moon in the solar system – it's bigger than Mercury!

2 Europa may have oceans of water under its icy surface, which could be home to alien life!

3 Triton has gassy **geysers** that could turn an astronaut into a frozen cube.

4 Io is covered in volcanoes, which send spurts of gas hundreds of kilometres into space!

5 Titan has some weird weather. Marble-sized raindrops fall to the ground as slowly as snowflakes do on Earth.

No place like home

Fancy visiting one of the planets of our solar system?
Be warned you might meet a gruesome end!

MERCURY:

Visit Mercury,
the closest
planet to the
Sun. There are
no clouds so every day
is sunny!

HEALTH HAZARD:

Bring a hard hat, so that
incoming space rubble
doesn't hit your head!

VENUS:

Enjoy days
that are
longer than
years, on a planet
that's almost exactly
the same size as Earth!

HEALTH HAZARD:

Travellers risk getting
roasted by temperatures
twice as hot as an oven.

MARS:

The red planet has the highest
volcanoes in the solar system,
and it never rains!

HEALTH HAZARD:

The air is mainly **carbon dioxide**, which
is poisonous to people.

JUPITER:

Gaze down on the beautiful swirling surface of the biggest planet in the solar system.

HEALTH HAZARD:

Violent storms and a smell of rotten eggs may put some travellers off.

URANUS:

Adventure seekers will love the only planet that spins around the Sun on its side.

HEALTH HAZARD:

Night in some places lasts for more than 40 Earth years, so be sure to pack candles.

SATURN:

Wow your friends with photos of Saturn's sparkly rings.

HEALTH HAZARD:

Watch out for giant ice storms, and high winds.

NEPTUNE:

Escape the crowds and visit beautiful blue Neptune, the furthest planet from the Sun.

HEALTH HAZARD:

Neptune is the windiest place in the solar system, with storms of up to 2,160 kilometres per hour!

Venus' surface

Mercury by day

Lead melts

Hot oven

Hottest temperature recorded on earth, in Libya

Earth's surface (average)

Ice

Temperature of freezer

Coldest temperature recorded on Earth in Antarctica

Saturn's cloud tops

Mercury by night

Oxygen freezes

Neptune's cloud tops

— 500

— 400

— 300

— 200

— 100

— 0

— −100

— −200

— −300

Dwarf planets

When it's a dwarf planet! Five dwarf planets have been named so far: Ceres, Pluto, Haumea, Makemake and Eris. They are hard to spot because they are small, and often very far from the Sun. These planets are roughly spherical, just like normal planets. They also follow their own path around the Sun (instead of orbiting another planet, like moons do).

Why don't they get the 'planet' badge?

Only planets can totally clear their path around the Sun. They do this by pulling in any object that comes close, either destroying it, or bashing it out of the way. Dwarf planets aren't big enough to do this.

Dwarf planet	Discovered	Did you know?
Ceres	1801	Ceres was classed as a planet and then an asteroid before it was finally called a dwarf planet.
Pluto	1930	Pluto has three moons.
Haumea	2003	Haumea is egg-shaped.
Makemake	2005	Makemake gets so cold in winter that its air freezes and falls to the ground!
Eris	2005	Eris takes 560 Earth years to orbit the Sun once.

Solar System Orbiter, August 2006

SHOCK AS PLUTO LOSES PLANET STATUS

It's bad news for fans of the solar system's ninth planet. Pluto has just been downgraded.

The International Astronomical Union (a big club for people who stare at the sky for a living) finally decided this month how to define a planet. They also invented a new class of solar system object: the dwarf planet.

Icy Pluto had been known as a planet since it was discovered in 1930. But its small size and odd-shaped path around the Sun got astronomers grumbling that it just didn't measure up. Pluto will now be known as a dwarf planet – and school textbooks from the last 76 years will have to be rewritten!

Pluto

Charon

Pluto's moon Charon is almost half the size of Pluto! Some space scientists think it should be called a dwarf planet too.

Asteroids and comets

What else is in the solar system?

After the solar system formed, there was a lot of rubble left over. Most is still zooming around the Sun, but sometimes a piece heads towards a planet and causes big trouble.

Asteroids

Billions of lumps of dusty rock called asteroids hang out between Mars and Jupiter. This **asteroid belt** has the worst traffic in the solar system – huge crashes happen all the time! As time passes, they are getting smashed into smaller and smaller pieces.

Scientists think there are more than a billion asteroids. Some are enough to wipe out a continent if they hit Earth.

Anyone who spots a new asteroid is allowed to name it! First you have to make sure that it's not one of the 200,000 that have already been discovered.

Comets

A huge cloud of icy comets circles our solar system. Sometimes one of these 'dirty snowballs' is nudged out of the cloud and zooms across the solar system. As it gets close to the Sun, the ice on the outside melts, forming a bright tail of gas and dust.

Don't set up camp on a comet. Every time it passes the Sun, more of the surface is melted away until it disappears!

Strange...

Every 500,000 years, a massive **meteorite** punches a hole around the size of London into Earth's surface. But this is nothing compared to the destruction caused when an asteroid hits Earth – just ask the dinosaurs!

... but true

Gravity is the glue!

What sticks the solar system together?

It takes a special kind of force to keep planets, moons, asteroids and comets orbiting around the Sun. That force is called gravity and it pulls objects together.

Do people have gravity?

Every object has gravity. The more massive an object is, the bigger its pull on other objects. The pull of gravity is also stronger if an object is closer. The Sun's gravity is much stronger than Earth's gravity, but because the Sun is further away, it's Earth that pulls you back down when you jump in the air.*

Top 5: useful effects of gravity

1. It stops you from floating off into space.

2. It makes things fall to the floor, from rain to footballs.

3. It keeps our atmosphere in place, so we always have air to breathe.

4. It keeps satellites in orbit, making mobile phones possible.

5. The Moon's gravity causes tides on Earth.

*Look back at pages 14 and 15 to see a photo of an astronaut on the moon.

Try this!

Can you find out if Earth's gravity pulls on some objects more than others?

What you need:

- three elastic bands
- a wooden rod
- two chairs
- three identical empty bubble bottles
- some modelling clay
- some feathers or tissue paper
- some rice or pasta
- some paper clips and thread

What to do:

1 Loop three elastic bands on to the wooden rod, and place it across two chairs.

2 Pack one bubble bottle with clay one with feathers or tissue paper, and one with rice or pasta. Fasten the lids.

3 Hang each container on an elastic band, using the paperclips and thread.

4 Earth's gravity pulls each container towards the centre of the planet. Which container is being pulled most strongly?

Hint: make sure each elastic band is exactly the same length and thickness, to make it a fair test.

The Universe

What is outside our solar system?

Our Sun and the planets are just a teeny, tiny part of the Universe. The Universe includes everything that exists, including billions of stars that hang around in huge groups called **galaxies**. Most are so far away, they can only be seen with powerful telescopes.

How big is the Universe?

It is so big that the distances would boggle your brain! Our solar system is a tiny neighbourhood in the Milky Way Galaxy. The next-nearest star in our galaxy is 40,000,000,000,000 (40 trillion) km away. A jet plane would take more than four and a half million years to make the trip (and that's not allowing for toilet breaks)!

Strange...

Stars are the 'cooking pots' of the Universe. The materials formed inside them zoom off into space when a star dies and become the building blocks for everything else in the Universe – including your body!

... but true

Solar system hunting

Scientists reckon there must be loads of other solar systems in the Universe. The Kepler Telescope is trying to spot planets orbiting other stars. When it finds one, it runs through a checklist to see if the planet is like Earth. Planets like ours would be the best places to look for alien life.

Kepler's checklist looks like this:

❑ Is the planet one-half to twice the size of the Earth?

❑ Does it travel around its star at the right distance (not too hot, and not too cold, so liquid water might exist)?

❑ Is there somewhere to buy lunch? (Ok, this one is not really part of Kepler's mission!)

Glossary

asteroid large lump of rock and metal that orbits the Sun

asteroid belt the area of space where most asteroids are found

astronomer scientist who studies stars, planets and anything else to do with space

atmosphere layer of gases around a planet

axis an imaginary line that runs straight through the centre of a planet, around which the planet turns

carbon dioxide gas found in small quantities in Earth's air, but which is poisonous to humans in large quantities

galaxies huge collections of stars held together by gravity

geysers jets of gas or liquid rising into the air from a hole in the ground

meteorite lump of rock or metal that falls to Earth from space

orbits moves around something in a fixed path

phases different shapes of the sunlit side of the Moon or a planet when seen from Earth

rovers unmanned vehicles used to explore the surface of a planet

space probes unmanned spacecrafts sent to explore space, and send information back to scientists on Earth

Index